HEALTHY
NOT OBSESSED

HOW VEGANISM CHANGED MY LIFE

VICTORIA MEURET

Tellwell Talent
www.tellwell.ca

ISBN
978-0-22880-865-7 (Paperback)

FOREWORD BY CARLY COOPER, LICENSED CLINICAL SOCIAL WORKER

It is currently estimated that about 8 million people suffer from an eating disorder in the US, and nearly half of Americans know someone suffering from an eating disorder (ED). Beyond this, though, far more people engage in what is called disordered eating (DE). At best, "normal eating" is when one can maintain a balanced diet and stop eating when full. Eating when bored or stressed, restrictive eating behaviors, and any anxiety around eating fall into the category of disordered eating.

Today's young adults are under a great deal of pressure to present an idealized version of themselves on social media and with peers. Our society's stubborn focus on extreme thinness, ultimate fitness and Photoshopped standards of beauty provides a perfect breeding ground for disordered eating in teens who are naturally looking to build their adult sense of self.

For those struggling with either an ED or DE, thoughts about calories, meals, taste and food avoidance can become obsessive. This mental state usually affects the person's relationships, ability to focus, self-esteem and sleep habits. An important distinction between an ED and DE is whether those affected can function in their normal environments. If they are not able to attend school, family functions or go out with friends because of food and eating concerns, they should seek professional guidance.

Victoria's approach is remarkable. She very clearly took pause when she noticed early warning signs and built her own strategies for maintaining a healthy weight and sense of self. At the same time, she worked on decreasing her anxiety around weight, health and exercise. Her recipes are easy, family-friendly and balanced. Best of all, she shares her struggles through a lens of both humility and empowerment, making it inviting for others to follow her lead .

Carly Cooper is a liscensed social worker in St.Louis, Missouri. She specializes in trauma, depression, anxiety, Family stress, and parenting.

INTRODUCTION

I have nothing against diets. They inspire people to be healthier and make a change for the better. It's when a diet becomes all you think about that it becomes a problem. In the course of my experience with diets, I've found I'm not the kind of person who can just dip my toe in the water to test things out. When I'm in, I'm all in.

I grew up in an environment where how I looked mattered, whether I liked it or not. I was a competitive gymnast for ten years. During those years I never once worried about what I ate or how I looked because I worked out every day for five hours without fail. When gymnastics had finally run its course and it was time to quit, I started working out at the gym and worrying about carbs, sugar content, and calories—not realizing how dangerously close I hovered between wanting to be healthy and wanting to be "perfect."

Before I knew it, food was the only thing on my mind. I would've given anything to be someone who didn't care what they ate, someone who could start a diet and give up. My perseverance proved a weakness and I couldn't give up control. It was time to make a change.

Food was no longer allowed to take up space in my head and I had a plan. I had to re-learn how to eat, and do so without worrying about ruining all of my "progress." This is when I went vegan. I saw how this lifestyle had helped so many other people who struggle the same way I do and I wanted what they had. At first, it worried everyone around me because they thought I was just funneling all of my unhealthy, restrictive eating habits into a new, similarly unhealthy diet. It took me a while to figure out what it meant for me to be healthy.

My dad taught me that everyone needs a formula: a list of values and practices one must maintain in order to nurture their mental health. For me, this formula consists of a consistent workout regime (consistent not ruthless), a strong relationship with God, and spending quality time with the people around me. It took a long time to figure out my formula, but it was the best thing I could have done for myself. As long as I balance these three things, I can be the best version of myself. It no longer matters if I am "perfect" or not; I just want to be healthy and happy. The girl who can make anyone laugh and not care if I look stupid. I wanted to go back to the person who put God first, because in the midst of my self-obsession, I had managed to cut Him out. Disordered eating doesn't only affect you. It affects your family, your friends—everyone who knows and cares about you. I realized I had cut off relationships that meant the world to me. Disordered eating is a selfish disease that takes up all of your free time *if you let it.* Will you?

I decided to write this book for other people who silently struggle with food because they don't think they need to change. If this is you, I cannot emphasize enough how wrong that is. This is an illness that, if let off the leash, rampages lives, marriages, families, and careers. However, unlike a disease of the body, this is something that can be healed. Something that can be controlled and tamed. I wanted to share each phase I went through as I crawled back to the person I once was, and to the God I feared would have left me by now.

It may sound counter-intuitive to write a cookbook when for years I had a serious fear of eating what I made. But, surprisingly, cooking became the therapy I needed, and it revealed to me that I was missing out on so much of life by depriving myself of the joy that comes with making something from scratch, and *tasting* it. The pride you feel when you taste something you made with your hands—it's unmatched. For so long I let myself miss out on a whole side of life that now brings me so much joy and comfort. The reason I made a vegan cookbook was to show the newfound pride I have in food. With each recipe in this book, I tweaked ingredients, and made dish my own. While cooking is something that I do for enjoyment and pastime, I wanted to share this with my readers because I am asked several times a day: "What do vegans eat besides lettuce?" and "Is chicken vegan?". To my friends: now you know exactly what vegans eat!

In a medical context, disordered eating is not life-threatening, but for those who are dealing with it, it can be all-consuming. The back-and-forth between only allowing yourself to eat "healthy" and not giving two craps about what you eat leads to a vicious cycle that never seems to end. My goal for this book is to share my journey to becoming healthy, not obsessed.

THE TRUTH ABOUT "HEALTHY"

The ugly truth is that making the decision to have a healthy state of mind is the easiest part. Things get difficult when it's time to make a decision between how you were in the past and how you want to be in the future. Everyday choices you make to step out of old patterns are what move you forward. Each time I let myself slip the slightest bit, I would lose sight of why I wanted to change in the first place. Don't worry—it won't always be like this, and it won't take up this much space in your head when you follow through on the promise you made to yourself to change.

I used to be obsessed with only eating fruit every day until noon. I had read somewhere that it helps with digestion and gives the body a nice kick start to the day, and I thought since I was being consistent and eating a good amount of fruit that I was in the clear. I realized I had a problem when I went on vacation and the only fruit available was a green banana. It made me want to cry knowing I would have to stray from routine, and this was exactly my problem. I was eating healthy without a healthy mindset.

It's easy to come across as someone who has it all together. When I was struggling with my own eating habits, I actually had people coming to me for nutrition advice—and that scared me. I couldn't be sure that I was giving them sound advice since I was struggling so much on my own. This also made me realize that more people deal with this than I ever could have imagined. My advice to anyone who is struggling is to figure out why you are doing this to yourself and determine if it is coming from a place of self-hate or a need for perfection. Until you learn the difference between wanting be someone else entirely and wanting to improve the person you already are, you have no business diving into those deep waters. Identify the honest reason you are hurting yourself and be accountable. Believe me, truly loving yourself is a gift. Hold on to that, and you are already mentally stronger for it.

EATING OUT

For me, the most difficult part of eating out was seeing how carefree other people seemed to be. They could be spontaneous and unplanned; meanwhile, I had always looked at the menu ahead of time and already decided what I would order before I got there. This is obviously not a normal thing to do and, over time, I stopped allowing myself to look at the menu in advance. Being spontaneous scared me because the idea that I would eat something I hadn't planned or budgeted for threw me off my game.

I was out one day with my friends when they decided we should make a pit stop at Starbucks. This is such a normal, everyday thing for most people that used to bring me so much anxiety. I ordered something in spite of myself because I didn't want my friends to worry about me, and that's when I realized something: A year from now, I won't remember the extra calories I ate one day or the cheat meal I wasn't supposed to have. I will remember the time I spent and the fun I had with those around me. If I said no to these opportunities to go out and share a meal, I would only remember the chances I didn't take.

BODY IMAGE

As women, we naturally seek the beauty in life. We fine-tune the details of our weddings down to the thickness of the invitations, and we paint our toenails even though we are the only people who really care what our feet look like. Women strive to be and feel beautiful, and this is a special and wonderful thing. Yet it so easily turns rotten and appearance becomes something we worship. Whether we realize it or not, we consistently put our physical appearance above other things that really matter in life.

In my case, I was severely deprived of nutrients and the self-love my body so badly needed. I was always comparing myself to other women, letting myself believe they were more desirable than I was. On top of my disordered eating, the *need to feel desired* overwhelmed me. I wanted to be wanted. This is not something I'm proud of. It took time and mentoring for me to realize that it was not humble of me to think I was ugly, but rather arrogant to believe that as beautiful as creation is around me, I was an exception. How ignorant of me to think I was the only ugly, imperfect thing God had created.

I challenged myself every day to change this twisted view I had of myself. Each morning, I forced myself to look in the mirror and find one thing about my appearance that I loved. Not just something I thought was cute, but something I *loved*. I found things I had been overlooking for years, like the lock of hair on my forehead that curls just like Superman's. The fact that my teeth are naturally straight and aligned. Every day, I became more grateful for the body I was given and realized the ugliness I felt was not external. The real bitterness and unworthy thoughts were sprouting from my issues with food. As I progressed, the happy outgoing person I was (the person I missed) was slowly revived.

THERE IS NOTHING WRONG WITH YOU,

It really surprised me to find out how many other people were dealing with the same thing I was. There is such a stigma around mental illness and it's appalling. When a person is diagnosed with cancer, we can all find it in our hearts to have sympathy and help that person carry the burden of being sick. Yet, we tend to write off people with mental health issues as "crazy" or lost causes. There is nothing wrong with admitting you don't feel your best. Left unchecked, damaged mental health and self-esteem can be just as devastating as a fatal disease. I hid my struggles from my family for years because I didn't want to be seen as a disappointment. A screw-up. How could I have made something so simple this complicated?

About a year ago, things were going really well and I was beginning to understand what being balanced meant. For a split second, I was someone who could have cheat meals and enjoy them, and get ice cream with my family without my anxiety crapping on our fun. Then came Christmas 2017, when I had surgery. I wasn't allowed to move for months, let alone exercise. I told myself it wouldn't be a problem and that I could handle food being the only thing in my control. Man, was I wrong.

Now the only thing I could think about was food. For the first time, I had to deal with my relationship with food head-on. Over and over, I told myself, "It's just food. Even supermodels eat." In order to heal from my surgery, I was told my caloric intake *needed* to increase for my body to recover. This gave me the chance to realize how damaging my habits were because I almost didn't want to give my body what it needed. I thought I would almost rather not fully recover than gain five pounds. On a daily basis, I was denying my body the basic nutrition it needed to function. This experience made me stronger in the end because it forced me to look my demons in the eye and heal my relationship with food—something I can honestly say I never planned on doing. I am not saying I am completely and magically healed. Yes, I have learned to manage my thoughts about food, but I don't think I will ever be able to erase the trauma that years of living with this mentality has left me with—and that's okay.

Today, I can say that I am fully committed to becoming healthy, not obsessed, and I will never go back to my old ways of denying my body and soul what it needs. I refuse to let food win, and the peace of mind knowing that food will never again control my life is so worth the effort it took to change my thinking patterns and eating habits. Everyone deserves this peace of mind.

BREAKFAST MUNCH

TROPICAL HEMP SMOOTHIE BOWL

Starting your morning off with the antioxidants in strawberries and mango, along with the healthy carbs in bananas and almond milk, will give you lasting energy and a good start to your day! The hemp and chia seeds supply healthy omega-3 fats that provide the satiation that should come with breakfast. Serves: 1

Ingredients:

1 ½ frozen bananas
1 Tbsp. hemp seeds
1 sliced Ataulfo mango

1 cup almond milk
1 cup frozen strawberries
1 Tbsp. chia seeds

Toppings (Optional):

Granola
Coconut chips (sweetened or unsweetened)
Cacao nibs
Strawberries (fresh sliced)

Directions:

1. Add all ingredients into a blender, and blend until the mixture is one solid color. If there are still frozen bananas or strawberries left unblended, it is not ready yet.
2. Pour into a medium-sized bowl and add toppings that you fancy! Eat immediately for your enjoyment!

SIX-INGREDIENT PANCAKES

Pancakes are a classic American start to the day. While they are absolutely delicious, this sweet breakfast does not need to be heavy and complicated! This recipe contains the energy you need to start your day with a clear head and a healthy heart! Serves: 1

Ingredients:

1 cup old-fashioned oats   1 Tbsp. apple cider vinegar
1 cup almond milk   1 Tbsp. baking soda
1 medium-large ripe banana   1 Tbsp. pure maple syrup

Optional Additions:

2 tsp. cinnamon   ¼ cup pumpkin puree
1 Tbsp. cacao powder

Directions:

1. Preheat your griddle to 350°F. (If using a skillet, turn the burner to medium heat.)
2. Add all ingredients to a high-speed blender, and combine until a smooth mixture is achieved.
3. Set mixture aside for 2 minutes to thicken before pouring onto heat. Grease pan with coconut oil, and cook about 1 minute on each side.

Notes:

Cinnamon is a great addition to these pancakes, as it has powerful anti-inflammatory properties and a homemade flavor! This recipe is a good base for any flavors you wish to add, including the healthy options listed above!

VEGAN FROZEN MOCHA

For most adults, coffee in the morning is essential. However, there is no need to leave your kitchen to get that sweet, caffeinated pick-me-up! This recipe contains all-natural ingredients that will not lead to the notorious drop in energy that comes with traditional coffee! Serves: 1

Ingredients:

2 medium frozen bananas
2 Tbsp. cacao powder
2 Tbsp. instant coffee
1 Tbsp. pure maple or
    agave syrup
¾ to 1 cup almond milk

Directions:

1. Add all the ingredients to a high-speed blender and combine until a smooth consistency is achieved.
2. Enjoy on the go!

GREEN POWER SMOOTHIE

Getting your greens in the morning is the smart way get your five veggies a day! Making yourself a big green smoothie will give your immune system a boost with its healthy ingredients and the option to add any extras that you want! Mix it up!

Ingredients:

2 medium frozen bananas

2 handfuls raw spinach

1 ½ cups almond milk

1 cup fresh berries of your choice

Optional Additions:

1 packet frozen acai

1-2 tsp. hemp seeds

1 scoop vanilla protein powder

1 tsp. maca powder

1 Tbsp. wheatgrass powder

Directions:

1. Place the spinach and almond milk in a high-speed blender and pulse until spinach is fully combined.
2. Add the rest of the ingredients to the blender (this way there won't be any large pieces of spinach in the final product)!

Notes:

The more frozen ingredients you use, the more of an ice-cream consistency you will have. This recipe also tastes great if room-temperature bananas are your preference.

CLASSIC WAFFLES

This would not be a true cookbook if waffles were not included! This recipe is a twist on the classic. Tweak them to make them your own, and get creative with how you serve these fluffy favorites!

Ingredients:

2 Tbsp. melted coconut oil
1-2 tsp. vanilla extract
1 ¼ cup almond milk
1 ¼ cup flour (any kind works)

2 tsp. baking powder
3 Tbsp. coconut sugar (any sweetener of your choice works fine)
¼ tsp. salt

Directions:

1. Preheat waffle iron to medium-high heat
2. Combine all the wet ingredients in a medium bowl and set aside.
3. In a separate large bowl, combine the dry ingredients, and make a well in the center.
4. Pour the wet ingredients into the well of dry ingredients and fold ingredients until combined but not overmixed.
5. Grease waffle iron, and add ¼ cup of batter, or enough to fill iron.
6. Following waffle iron directions, cook until ready, then place on cooling rack to allow waffles to get crispy.
7. Add fun toppings and share with the ones you love!

Notes:

I usually use whole wheat flour for this recipe, but any flour will work! I have used oat flour, buckwheat flour, and all-purpose white flour in the past. The results will vary in texture, but not in flavor.

OIL-FREE CREPES

A lighter alternative to the original crepe that does not sacrifice flavor or enjoyment! Enjoy a wholesome, delicious breakfast and treat yourself!

Ingredients:

1 medium/large ripe banana

1 cup flour (any kind will work)

1 cup water

1 tsp. baking powder

2 Tbsp. brown sugar

A pinch of salt

Optional Additions:

¼ cup dairy-free chocolate chips

1 cup fresh sliced strawberries

¼ cup maple syrup

Dusting of powdered sugar

Directions:

1. Mix all ingredients in a blender and grease and preheat skillet to medium-high heat.
2. Pour ½ cup batter on skillet and spread as thin as possible for best results!
3. Cook until the edges begin to lift up, or the crepe is easy to flip. This will take about 2-3 minutes for each side.
4. Place add-ons inside and fold, top with maple syrup or powdered sugar and enjoy while they're hot!

VEGAN FRENCH TOAST

This recipe contains healthy carbs and the perfect sweetness! Spice it up and make it your own! Using older bread will give it a crunchier finish and absorb more flavor.

Ingredients:

1 large banana
1 Tbsp. agave nectar
¾ cup full-fat coconut milk
2 tsp. vanilla extract
1 tsp. cinnamon

2 Tbsp. dairy-free butter
   (e.g. Earth Balance)
   for frying
5-6 slices day-old bread

Toppings:

½ cup fresh fruit of your choice
Dusting of powdered sugar

Directions:

1. Preheat your skillet to medium-high heat.
2. Add the banana, coconut milk, vanilla extract, cinnamon and agave to a blender and combine completely.
3. Pour mixture into a large bowl, making the mixture shallow rather than deep.
4. Add vegan butter to the preheated skillet, and spread evenly.
5. When the butter is hot, dip each slice of bread into mixture so that both sides are evenly coated.
6. Cook on each side until golden brown.
7. Serve hot with desired toppings!

BERRY PROTEIN SMOOTHIE

It's important to include protein in every meal to get the full feeling we need to sustain us throughout the day and keep us from eating unhealthy snacks . Smoothies are an easy way to get protein with all the powders and supplements we can add these days! You will undoubtedly enjoy this variation on a fruity start to your day!

Ingredients:

1 ½ large, ripe bananas (the riper, the better)

1 serving vanilla protein powder

1 cup frozen or fresh mixed berries

1 ½ cups almond milk

Directions:

1. Add all ingredients to blender and blend on high speed. (I use the NutriBullet.)
2. Take it with you to go, or pour into a bowl and add fun and interesting toppings!
3. Enjoy immediately for best results.

Notes:

For those who prefer their smoothies cold, using frozen fruit is the best way to go! Adding ice works, also, but it changes the texture and dilutes the natural sweetness of fruit. I have also tried this recipe with rice milk, water, coconut water, and even watermelon juice! All of these worked fine—almond milk just gave it the creamiest texture in my opinion!

POWER OATS

Oats are an underestimated food. They lower cholesterol, aid digestion, and help control blood sugar levels! Here is a simple and delicious way to incorporate this superfood into your everyday diet.

Ingredients:

½ cup old-fashioned oats

1 cup almond milk

2 tsp. cinnamon

1 tsp. vanilla extract

1 Tbsp. pure maple syrup

1 small apple, chopped

Directions:

1. Pour the oats and almond milk in a saucepan on medium heat. Allow to boil before adding cinnamon, vanilla, and maple syrup.
2. Once the mixture is starting to absorb, add the chopped apple.
3. Serve hot and enjoy the delicious sustainable energy!

VEGAN BANANA BREAD

Going vegan does not mean you have to sacrifice your favorites! Banana bread has been a family favorite in my house since I can remember, and I wanted to keep my peeps happy! Treat yourself to this indulgent morning treat!

Ingredients:

1 cup white sugar

1 ½ cups mashed banana (bananas should be very ripe)

½ cup coconut oil

2 tsp. vanilla extract

¼ cup almond milk

1 tsp. apple cider vinegar

2 cups flour (gluten-free options work also)

¼ tsp. salt

¾ tsp. baking soda

Directions:

1. Preheat your oven to 350° F, and grease a 9x5 inch loaf pan.
2. Combine the mashed banana, sugar, coconut oil and vanilla extract until most lumps are gone. Some lumps are good.
3. Stir in apple cider vinegar and almond milk. After fully mixed, fold in the rest of the ingredients until no flour is left on sides of the bowl.
4. Pour into greased pan and bake for 1 hour, or until you can insert a toothpick and it comes out clean.
5. Allow to cool for 15 minutes on cooling rack before eating!

VEGAN BREAKFAST BURRITOS

For those who favor a savory breakfast, this is the perfect recipe for you! It's packed with healthy fats, vegetables, protein, and carbohydrates! You will not regret giving this recipe a go!

Ingredients:

¼ cup chopped bell pepper (color of your choice)

2 Tbsp. diced red onion

2 tsp. minced garlic

2 chopped large mushrooms

1 pkg. extra firm tofu (pressed preferred—can press it yourself)

½ tsp. each: cumin, chili pepper, salt and pepper

2 medium tortillas

½ avocado, sliced evenly

6 cherry tomatoes, sliced in half

2 Tbsp. hummus (flavor of your choice)

2 handfuls spring mix salad

Directions:

1. The first five ingredients make up the tofu scramble. Sauté all veggies and tofu in ¼ cup of water on high heat until soft. Add spices when only a little water is left at the bottom of the pan. Once fully combined, remove from heat.
2. Place half of the tofu mixture in the center of a tortilla, and assemble with half of the tomatoes, avocado, spring mix and hummus.
3. Enjoy warm!

Notes:
This recipe also pairs well with salsa!

LEMON BLUEBERRY MUFFINS

The closest you can get to eating dessert for breakfast! Makes 12, so share these with friends! They're hard not to love.

Ingredients:

1 cup soy/almond milk

1 Tbsp. apple cider vinegar

¼ cup plus 2 Tbsp. coconut oil

2 cups flour (I use all-purpose for this recipe)

½ cup plus 2 Tbsp. granulated sugar

2 ½ tsp. baking powder

¼ tsp. baking soda

½ tsp. salt

2 tsp. vanilla extract

1 Tbsp. lemon extract or zest from one lemon

2 cups frozen wild blueberries

Directions:

1. Preheat oven to 375°F.
2. In a small bowl, combine plant milk and apple cider vinegar and set aside for five minutes to curdle.
3. In a medium-sized bowl, combine the oil, sugar, lemon zest, vanilla extract, and soy milk mixture. Set aside.
4. In a large bowl, combine all dry ingredients, then add the soy milk mixture and stir, but not too much. A few lumps are okay.
5. Pour into a greased muffin tin and cook for about 20 minutes. Cool for 10 minutes before serving.

CINNAMON GRANOLA

Granola can be used as a topping and a cereal! This recipe gives a pleasant crunch to yogurt, smoothie bowls, and so much more! I keep a big glass jar of this granola on hand at all times. I know you will love this recipe!

Ingredients:

2 cups old-fashioned oats

1 cup chopped nuts of your choice

1-1 ½ Tbsp. ground cinnamon

¼ cup all-natural peanut butter (or other nut butter), melted

½ cup pure maple syrup

¼ tsp. sea salt

Directions:

1. Preheat your oven to 325°F.
2. Add the dry ingredients to a large bowl and set aside.
3. Melt peanut butter (or nut butter of your choice) until smooth and creamy. Mix together with the maple syrup and pour over the dry ingredients. Leave no oats uncovered!
4. Spread evenly on a cookie sheet with parchment paper, and bake for 15 minutes, then remove from oven to stir around. Return to oven for about 15 more minutes, or until the mixture is golden brown and crunchy.
5. Allow to cool before serving, and enjoy!

Notes:

Adding 2 Tbsp. of coconut oil will result in a crunchier end product, but the oil-free version is just as delicious!

CHERRY PROTEIN SMOOTHIE

Simplicity is key!

Ingredients:

1 ½ cups frozen cherries

1 cup almond milk (sweetened or unsweetened)

1 serving vanilla protein powder

1 medium/large frozen banana

1 tsp. maca powder

1 Tbsp. hemp seeds, hulled

Optional Toppings:

Coconut chips

Goji berries

Almond butter

Sliced fresh fruit

Dairy-free yogurt

Directions:

1. In a blender, blend all ingredients at high-speed until smooth.
2. Enjoy in a bowl with fancy toppings, or on the go!

CHOCOLATE POWER SHAKE

It is a myth that vegans lack protein sources and can't gain muscle. This recipe is a perfect pre/post-workout protein boost!

Ingredients:

1 cup coconut milk

1 scoop chocolate
   protein powder

½ cup fresh blueberries

One large handful spinach

1 medium frozen banana

1 Tbsp. almond butter

Optional:

Cacao nibs

Cacao powder

Directions:

1. Pulse at high speed in blender until smooth.
2. Best enjoyed immediately.

LUNCH/DINNER MUNCH

VEGAN "MAC AND CHEESE"

All the flavor with none of the cruelty! Enjoy this American classic in a new and inventive way!

Ingredients:

1 cup soaked cashews
1 cup water
¼ cup nutritional yeast
½ tsp. lemon juice
½ tsp. turmeric

1 tsp. garlic powder
1 tsp. salt
2 servings cooked whole
    wheat penne pasta

Optional:

Paprika or cilantro for garnish
Kale (on the side)

Directions:

1. Pour cashews into a bowl and cover with warm water. Allow to sit for at least 1 hour. Transfer to blender along with all other ingredients and blend at high speed.
2. Boil pasta according to box instructions and strain.
3. Pour desired amount of "cheese" sauce over the pasta and enjoy while it is hot! Garnish with paprika, cilantro, or more nutritional yeast for an extra punch of flavor!

TOFU NUGGETS

Ingredients:

1 pkg. extra firm tofu
½ cup bread crumbs
1 tsp. garlic powder
¼ cup nutritional yeast

2 Tbsp. coconut oil
2 Tbsp. cornstarch
4 Tbsp. water
Salt and pepper to taste

Optional:

Mixed herbs
Onion powder

Directions:

1. In a medium bowl, mix together bread crumbs, garlic powder, nutritional yeast, salt and pepper, (and mixed herbs and onion powder, if you like).

2. In a separate small bowl, combine cornstarch and water, and allow to thicken slightly.

3. Press tofu between 2 paper towels to remove some moisture. Cut the block into rectangles.

4. Heat a skillet on medium-high heat and add coconut oil.

5. Coat each rectangle of tofu in cornstarch mixture, and then in bread crumb mixture.

6. Fry on both sides until golden brown and crispy. Allow to cool before serving with ketchup or BBQ sauce!

CREAMY TOMATO PASTA

To get a dish this good, you don't have to slave for hours in the kitchen! It takes about 20 minutes from start to finish!

Ingredients:

5 servings cooked whole wheat shell pasta

2 cups pure tomato sauce

1 cup soaked cashews

1 cup water

1 whole garlic clove

2 tsp. salt

Pepper to taste

Directions:

1. Cook shell pasta according to box instructions.
2. Combine cashews, water, garlic, salt, and pepper in a food processor until a smooth, creamy texture is achieved.
3. Transfer cooked pasta, tomato sauce and cashew sauce into a skillet and allow to simmer. Once fully incorporated, it is ready to serve!

Notes:

Garnish using green onions, cilantro, salt and pepper, or parsley. This dish can be changed around to your liking and serves as a great base.

TACO BOWL

This recipe is quick and delicious! It's easy to add seasonings and toppings to make it your own!

Ingredients:

2 handfuls romaine lettuce, washed

½ cup cooked white or brown rice

½ cup black beans, drained and rinsed

½ cup canned corn, drained and rinsed

⅓ block extra firm tofu

½ packet taco seasoning

Directions:

1. Take the tofu out of the packaging and pat excess water dry. Cut into small rectangles and let sit on paper towel for 5 minutes.
2. Heat a non-stick pan on medium-high heat, and toast the tofu until all sides are crispy and golden brown. Add 2 Tbsp. water to the pan along with the taco seasoning. Allow the tofu to absorb the seasoning, then remove pan from heat.
3. Take the corn and black beans and heat in microwave for 1 minute to warm.
4. In a large salad bowl, place romaine lettuce in first, then the rice, and beans and corn last.

Notes:

I find that adding my favorite salsa on top ties the whole dish together. Other good additions would be guacamole, nutritional yeast, or dairy-free sour cream! Have fun customizing this delightful Mexican dish!

FRESH SPRING ROLLS

Those who know me, know that spring rolls are a staple in my diet! They are a great way to eat your vegetables and are simple to prepare! I know you will love the fresh taste of this traditional Vietnamese dish!

Ingredients:

6 sheets rice paper
1 small or ½
   a large cucumber
¾ cup shredded carrots
¼ cup chopped basil

¼ cup fresh mint
1 serving cooked thin
   rice noodles
2 large handfuls spring
   mix salad

Peanut Sauce:

¼ cup smooth natural
   peanut butter
2 Tbsp. pure maple syrup

1 Tbsp. Thai chili sauce
1 Tbsp. hoisin sauce
2 Tbsp. water

Directions:

1. In a small saucepan, combine all ingredients for the peanut sauce, and mix over low heat until a creamy consistency is achieved.
2. For the spring rolls, cut cucumber in half lengthwise, about two inches long. Then finely chop basil and mint.
3. Place rice noodles in a bowl with warm water until softened.
4. Fill a pie pan with more warm water for rice paper.
5. Soak each sheet for about 15 seconds, then lay out sheets on a clean surface, place all ingredients in the middle, and roll up like a burrito. Serve with peanut sauce and enjoy!

MICROWAVE-FRIENDLY STIR-FRY

I am all about sneaking veggies into my dinners! This recipe is no different. Here is a delicious way to include colorful produce in a way that is not bland and unappetizing!

Ingredients:

3 cups frozen mixed veggies
½ cup instant rice
1 cup water
2 Tbsp. teriyaki sauce
Green onions for garnish

Directions:

1. First, prepare instant rice according to the box instructions. Be sure to cover the rice and water with a paper towel to avoid a microwave disaster!
2. Next, combine frozen mixed veggies and 2 Tbsp. water in a microwave-safe bowl, and cover with paper towel. Heat for 2 minutes, or until veggies are soft and warmed all the way through.
3. Place the cooked rice on a plate and put the cooked veggies on top! Finish this dish with the teriyaki sauce and chopped green onions for garnish.
4. Enjoy warm, or save for later! This recipe is good for advance meal prepping and leftovers.

BUDDHA BOWL

Another sneaky and delicious way to eat those vegetables!

Ingredients:

3 handfuls of your favorite salad mix

½ cup chickpeas, drained and rinsed

½ cup cooked quinoa

½ to ¾ cup shredded carrots

2 Tbsp. chopped cilantro

1 large handful bean sprouts

Dressing:

1 Tbsp. hoisin sauce

2 Tbsp. Thai chili sauce

1 Tbsp. tahini

1 Tbsp. lemon juice

1 Tbsp. pure maple syrup

Directions:

1. Start with the dressing. Add all dressing ingredients to a small bowl and whisk together until creamy, adding small amounts of water until desired consistency is achieved

2. Place salad mix in a large salad bowl, then add chickpeas, quinoa, carrots, and bean sprouts on top.

3. Drizzle dressing on top and garnish with cilantro!

Notes:

For the dressing, using peanut butter instead of tahini works just as well! Do not worry if tahini is unavailable to you.

VEGAN TACO NIGHT

Serves: 2

Ingredients:

4 small flour or
   corn tortillas
1 cup black beans, drained
   and rinsed
1 cup canned corn, drained
   and rinsed

¾ cup salsa
1 whole avocado, sliced
Salt and pepper to taste
Chopped cilantro
   for garnish

Directions:

1. Preheat oven to 425°F.
2. For crunchy tacos: Take a muffin tin and place it upside down. Fold the tortillas in the shape of a crunchy taco shell and toast until the tortillas hold shape and become crunchy (about 15-20 minutes).
3. Once removed from the oven, allow shells to cool.
4. Add black beans, corn, avocado and salsa to each taco.
5. Add chopped cilantro on top for a fresh taste and enjoy!

CORN CHOWDER

A dorm-friendly comfort food . . . I know you will love this one! Good for advance meal prepping and leftovers!

Ingredients:

½ cup canned corn, drained and rinsed

2 tbsp. cornstarch

1 tsp. vegetable broth

¼ cup sweet potato cubes

½ cup water

½ cup non-dairy milk

¼ cup chopped celery

Salt to taste

Directions:

1. Put cubed sweet potato in a microwave-safe bowl. Add 1 Tbsp. water and cover with paper towel. Heat in microwave on high for 3-5 minutes or until fork-tender.

2. Add remaining ingredients to the same bowl used to steam sweet potatoes, and microwave on high for 3-4 minutes.

3. Enjoy it while it is warm!

CAULIFLOWER FETTUCCINE PASTA

Veggies have a funny way of being secretly delicious, especially in this traditionally heavy dish! This recipe is also good for leftovers, and can be stored in the fridge for up to a week.

Ingredients:

3 cups chopped cauliflower   1 tsp. garlic powder
3 cloves garlic   1 tsp. onion powder
½ a yellow onion   2 Tbsp. fresh chopped basil
1 Tbsp. oil of choice   1 cup vegetable stock
2-4 Tbsp. nutritional yeast   Salt to taste
1 Tbsp. lemon juice

Directions:

1. In a skillet, sauté onions in oil until translucent. Add garlic and sauté for another 15-30 seconds.
2. Add cauliflower and vegetable stock to the skillet and steam for five minutes, covered.
3. Add skillet contents and remainder of ingredients to a blender and blend on high speed until a smooth, creamy consistency is achieved. Serve with your favorite pasta and garnish with cilantro if desired!

VEGAN FETTUCCINE ALFREDO PART TWO

Ingredients:

200 grams whole wheat
    fettuccine pasta
2 Tbsp. oil of your choice
1 white onion, sliced
4 cloves garlic, chopped
1 cup frozen peas
⅔ cup soaked cashews

1 cup almond
    milk (unsweetened)
½ cup water
3 Tbsp. nutritional yeast (or
    more for personal taste)
1 Tbsp. lemon juice
1 tsp. salt

Directions:

1. Boil pasta according to box instructions
2. Sauté sliced onions in oil over medium-high heat for about 8 minutes, then add frozen peas for 4 minutes. Set aside.
3. In a blender, combine cashews, almond milk, water, lemon juice, nutritional yeast and salt. Blend on high speed for 1 minute and 30 seconds or until a creamy consistency is achieved.
4. Add sauce to skillet of onions and peas, and simmer for 5 minutes until thick.
5. Add cooked pasta and evenly coat.
6. Garnish with cilantro if desired and enjoy!

SIMPLE CURRY

Ingredients:

2 tsp. Himalayan salt

2 medium cubed
   russet potatoes

1 Tbsp. olive oil

1 diced white onion

4 cloves minced garlic

2 tsp. cumin

1/4 tsp. cayenne

4 tsp. curry powder

1 tsp. ginger, grated

1 can diced tomatoes

1 can chickpeas, precooked

1 can peas

1 can lite coconut milk

Salt/pepper to taste

Directions:

1. Boil cubed potatoes in water with Himalayan salt and test for fork-tenderness. Strain when soft.

2. In a large saucepan, heat oil over medium heat, and sauté white onion and garlic. Once translucent and fragrant, add cumin, cayenne, curry powder, salt, pepper, ginger, peas and chickpeas

3. Once spices are evenly distributed, add coconut milk and diced tomatoes. Simmer for 10 minutes before adding strained potatoes.

4. Serve over rice with green onions as garnish.

BLACK BEAN BURGERS

Ingredients:

1 Tbsp. olive oil

1 whole diced white onion

3 minced garlic cloves

2 whole carrots, grated

1 tsp. cumin

1 tsp. cilantro

½ tsp. chili powder

2 cans black beans, drained and rinsed

1 Tbsp. soy sauce

½ cup quick oats

Salt/pepper to taste

Directions:

1. Heat oil in a medium skillet over medium-high heat.
2. Sauté the white onion, garlic, and salt and pepper until fragrant and tender. Next, add grated carrots and further sauté for one minute. Set aside.
3. Pour the drained and rinsed black beans in a medium bowl. Mash with potato masher until creamy and thick. Pour skillet mixture into the mashed black beans.
4. Once totally combined, add soy sauce and quick oats, and fold in the final ingredients. Form mixture into individual patties and arrange on baking sheet lined with parchment paper. Freeze for 30 minutes.
5. In another skillet, heat 1 Tbsp. oil on medium heat and place patties directly on heat. Cook on each side until surface is crispy.

BURRITOS

Serves: 2

Ingredients:

2 large tortillas
½ cup uncooked rice
1 cup water
3 Tbsp. taco seasoning

½ cup black beans, drained
 and rinsed
½ cup canned corn,
 drained and rinsed
½ cup refried beans

Optional Additions:

Salsa

Directions:

1. Start with the rice. Pour the rice, water, and taco seasoning into a medium saucepan and bring to a boil. Once boiling, allow to simmer until all water is absorbed and rice is fluffy and soft (about 20 minutes).

2. Assemble! On the tortilla, use a spoon to spread a generous amount of refried beans lengthwise in the center, and add ¼ cup of cooked rice. Next, carefully place black beans and corn on top before rolling it up.

3. Put desired amount of salsa in serving dish.

4. Optional: if you have a panini press, this is a great way to get a crispy exterior without having to fry your food. I used one for this recipe and it brought everything together so well.

SNACK ATTACK

WHOLE FOOD FRENCH FRIES

This snack is a wholesome alternative to the drive-through French fries we all hate to love. Feel free to add your own spices! This recipe is good for beginners and forgiving if every step is not followed perfectly.

Ingredients:

2 medium russet potatoes   2 tsp. Himalayan salt
1 Tbsp. garlic powder   1 Tbsp. coconut oil

Directions:

1. Preheat your oven to 425°F.
2. Slice potatoes into thin wedges, and soak in cold water for 30 minutes to remove some of the starch.
3. After soaking, put the wedges in a large bowl, and add coconut oil, garlic powder, and Himalayan salt. Toss with your hands until every wedge is evenly coated.
4. Spread the fries onto a cookie sheet lined with parchment paper, and bake in the oven for 20 minutes. Remove from oven to flip fries over and bake for another 20 minutes or until fries are golden brown and crispy.
5. Allow to cool partially before serving!

CHOCOLATE TRAIL MIX BARK

This on-the-go recipe is packed with delicious ingredients and provides the rich, chocolatey taste you crave with none of the guilt!

Ingredients:

¾ cup chopped vegan dark chocolate

2 Tbsp. coconut oil

1 cup dried cranberries

½ cup pistachios

½ cup sweetened shredded coconut

Directions:

1. In a microwave-safe bowl, combine vegan dark chocolate with coconut oil, and microwave in 30-second intervals until a thick, smooth consistency is achieved.
2. Line a cookie sheet with parchment paper. Spoon the chocolate sauce onto the cookie sheet to make discs that are about 1.5 inches in diameter.
3. While mixture is still wet, add a sprinkle of pistachios, dried cranberries and coconut shreds to the top of each disc.
4. Refrigerate until firm .
5. Store in a sealed container in the fridge for future snacking!

COOKIE DOUGH ENERGY BITES

They taste just as good as they sound! Give these a try the next time you think about buying a packaged energy bar—I promise you won't regret it! These bites will satisfy your snack cravings in that unbearable time between meals.

Ingredients:

⅔ cup creamy peanut butter

1 cup old-fashioned oats

2 Tbsp. pure maple syrup

¼ cup vegan chocolate chips

¼ cup flax seeds

¼ cup hemp seeds

Directions:

1. In a large bowl, add all of the ingredients and fold with a wooden spoon until everything is coated with peanut butter, and oats are evenly distributed.

2. Using a small ice cream scoop, scoop the dough and roll into ball shape using your hands.

3. Store in the refrigerator in a sealed container for up to a week!

CHOCOLATE CHIP COOKIES

Believe it or not, vegans can enjoy this classic treat! Everything can be eaten in moderation.

Ingredients:

2 cups flour

1 tsp. baking soda

1 tsp. baking powder

¼ - ½ tsp. salt

2 tsp. vanilla extract

1 cup packed brown sugar

½ cup vegetable oil

¾ cup chopped
    dark chocolate

Directions:

1. Preheat your oven to 350°F.
2. In a small bowl, combine brown sugar, oil, and vanilla. Set aside.
3. In a large bowl, add flour, salt, baking soda, and baking powder. With a hand mixer, pour liquid mixture into dry ingredients and mix well.
4. Fold in chocolate.
5. On a cookie sheet lined with parchment paper, using an ice cream scoop, portion out cookie dough and leave 1 ½ inches between each cookie.
6. Bake for 10-15 minutes.
7. Cool for 5 minutes before serving!

DECADENT VEGAN CHOCOLATE CAKE

Ingredients:

3 cups all-purpose flour

2 cups sugar

½ cup cocoa powder

Pinch of salt

1 Tbsp. baking powder

½ cup coconut oil (melted)

½ cup pure maple syrup

1 ½ cups almond milk

1 cup softened vegan butter

2 cups powdered sugar

2 tsp. vanilla extract

1 cup cocoa powder

¼ cup almond milk

Directions:

1. Preheat oven to 375°F, and grease two 9-inch round cake pans.
2. In a large mixing bowl, combine all dry ingredients and whisk together. Create a well in the center, and add coconut oil, maple syrup and almond milk. Whisk until combined but not overmixed.
3. Divide the batter evenly among the two greased pans, and bake for 30 minutes.
4. For the icing, using a hand mixer. Cream together vegan butter, powdered sugar, cocoa powder, vanilla extract and almond milk.
5. Once cakes have baked for 30 minutes, check for doneness by inserting a toothpick in the center. Once toothpick comes out clean, allow cakes to cool on a rack.
6. Remove cakes from pans. Place one on a serving plate and ice the top only, then place the second layer on top before icing the rest of the cake.
7. Store on counter in cake container for up to five days.

TWO-INGREDIENT VEGAN FUDGE

You heard right! Believe it or not, you only need two simple, easily accessible ingredients to make this classic treat!

Ingredients:

1 ½ cups creamy peanut butter

1 ½ cups dairy-free chocolate chips

Directions:

1. In a small saucepan, heat peanut butter and chocolate chips over low heat and stir constantly until completely melted. Remove from heat.
2. Grease a 9x9 inch pan. Pour fudge mixture into the pan and place in fridge until firm.
3. For best results, store on the counter in an airtight container for up to a week! Enjoy!

BROWNIES

Makes 12 servings.

Ingredients:

2 cups flour (all-purpose or other)

2 cups granulated sugar

¾ cup unsweetened cocoa powder/ cacao powder

1 tsp. baking powder

1 tsp. salt

1 cup coconut oil

1 cup warm water

2 Tbsp. vanilla extract

Directions:

1. Preheat your oven to 350°F.
2. In a large bowl, combine all ingredients and mix well.
3. Grease a 9x13 inch pan, and add brownie mixture.
4. Bake for 25-30 minutes, or until the surface is no longer shiny. Check with a toothpick for doneness, and make sure it comes out clean.
5. Cool for 15 minutes to allow to set before serving.

LEMONADE COCONUT CUPCAKES

These cupcakes are such a good summertime treat! They are great for parties and non-vegan approved! Everyone will love these.

Ingredients:

1 ½ cups soy milk (or any milk substitute)

1 Tbsp. apple cider vinegar

½ cup vegetable oil

2 tsp. vanilla extract

2 cups flour (all-purpose works best)

1 cup granulated sugar

¼ cup shredded coconut

2 tsp. baking powder

½ tsp. baking soda

½ tsp. salt

Directions:

1. Preheat oven to 350°F.
2. In a small bowl, combine milk substitute and apple cider vinegar, and set aside.
3. In another small bowl, mix together remaining wet ingredients and set aside. In a larger bowl, add all dry ingredients.
4. Next, add the milk mixture to the wet ingredients and mix well. Then pour into the dry mixture.
5. In a lined muffin tin, use an ice cream scoop to portion out batter.
6. Bake for 10-15 minutes, or until the top of the cupcakes are just starting to brown.
7. Cool for a few minutes before serving—these taste best served warm!

AUTHOR Q&A

1. What should a parent or loved one do if they suspect an eating disorder?

It is different for every person. It's hard to hear you have a problem from someone you love, so start by letting them know how much you will support them through the whole journey. You have to help your loved one realize for themselves that they have a problem in order for them to want to change.

2. How can you tell the difference between someone who is just trying to eat healthy, and someone who is using it as a platform for control?

It will always be about control. Instead of controlling the food itself, I had to learn to control my feelings about food. Whether I was eating animal protein or not, I was restricting which foods I could eat. Regardless of the diet I chose, the issues around control would still be there. I had to learn to control my feelings instead of the food.

3. As as a parent, how would I know the difference between healthy management of the anxiety around food and the eating disorder taking over?

Actions will always speak louder than words. The more someone says no to certain foods and food-related experiences, the more you should be concerned.

4. What do you mean by "food-related experiences"?

When a person frequently says no or has anxiety related to spontaneous food decisions (such as joining friends or family at a restaurant or café, without having planned it in advance), this may be a red flag. They react this way because they have not "budgeted" for that food for the day, and the loss of control is debilitating. They say no because they can't figure out how to make it work with their strict regime.

5. If I am concerned about my child, how can I have a conversation about this with them in a positive way?

There is no easy way to have the conversation. The best way to begin is to let them know that they are not broken, but their habits are. Then give them time to consider it, to really look at the fear and the facts and come to their own conclusion. Unless they get there with you, the conversation will go nowhere.

6. How does being vegan affect you socially? Does it hinder your ability to go out with friends and family?

Not at all. People are so quick to assume a vegan can only eat vegetables, and that eating out is no longer an option. No matter where I am, there is always something on the menu that I can eat. Sometimes I have to pick and choose from a few different things, but I can always figure it out.